Other titles in the series:
The World's Greatest Cat Cartoons
The World's Greatest Computer Cartoons
The World's Greatest Golf Cartoons

Published simultaneously in 1993 by Exley Publications
in Great Britain, and Exley Giftbooks in the USA.

Selection © Exley Publications Ltd.
The copyright for each cartoon remains with the cartoonist.

ISBN 1-85015-461-9

Front cover illustration by Roland Fiddy.
Designed by Pinpoint Design.
Edited by Mark Bryant.
Printed and bound by Grafo, S.A. – Bilbao, Spain.

Exley Publications Ltd, 16 Chalk Hill, Watford, Herts WD1 4BN,
United Kingdom.
Exley Giftbooks, 359 East Main Street, Suite 3D, Mount Kisco, NY
10549, USA.

THANK YOU

We would like to thank all the cartoonists who submitted entries for *The World's Greatest DAD CARTOONS*. They came in from many parts of the world - including Greece, Yugoslavia, Ireland, the United Kingdom and the USA.

Special thanks go to the cartoonists whose work appears in the final book. They include Sally Artz page 38; Les Barton page 69; Eric Burgin page 41; Hector Breeze page 62; Martha Campbell pages 16, 30; Roland Fiddy cover, title page and pages 5, 9, 17, 18, 19, 35, 36, 57, 64; Finbow page 8; Toni Goffe pages 25, 37, 73; Bud Grace page 71; Alex Graham pages 12, 24, 33, 39, 44, 51; Bud Handelsman page 40; Merrily Harpur pages 4, 49; David Hawker page 72; Michael Heath pages 14, 15, 65, 68, 74; Martin Honeysett page 75; Tony Husband page 7; Anthony Hutchings page 58; Vernon Kirby page 53; Larry pages 20, 66, 77; Norman Mansbridge page 55; Henry Martin page 76; David Myers pages 10, 11, 22, 23, 34, 45, 54, 56; Pantelis Palios page 5; Ken Pyne page 63; Bryan Reading page 48; Frank Rodgers pages 26, 27, 29, 70; Albert Rusling page 21; Davor Stambuk page 28; Bill Stott pages 31, 67; J. W. Taylor pages 50, 52; Taylor page 59; Norman Thelwell pages 13, 79; Thos page 32; Jim Unger pages 42, 43, 46, 47, 60, 61; Mike Williams page 78.

Every effort has been made to trace the copyright holders of cartoons in this book. However any error will gladly be corrected by the publisher for future printings.

THE WORLD'S GREATEST

DAD

CARTOONS

EDITED BY
Mark Bryant

EXLEY
MT. KISCO, NEW YORK · WATFORD, UK

"Just think — one day whoever's in there will be scorning all my little jokes."

"She's got your wrinkles!"

"It's no good! Unless you can look like Yogi Bear you'd better give it up!"

"Must you do that every time I wash?"

"*Now this one's a Lulu — watch what happens when your father kicks sand in this man's face…*"

"Please don't stop just because I happen to come in
after a particularly tiring day at the office."

"Give it to me — it's child-proof."

"Mummy! Mummy! Daddy's batteries have run out!"

"Yes, Patricia. I think it's safe to confess without your lawyer present."

"Guess who's been made cockroach monitor?"

"I think this is *it*!"

"Do you mind if my friends watch?"

"How did the dance go?"

"It wasn't a man's world for long, was it, Dad?"

"Quick! Fall down and hurt your knee. My dad's coming
and I fancy an ice-cream!"

"You're not sitting on my frogs, I hope!"

"You deliberately chopped that worm into two!"

TONI GOFFE

"Relax Dad. It's just my homework.
I didn't want it to get wet!"

"How can you communicate with someone who never watches the commercials!"

"Does your dad keep going on about some stuff that doesn't grow on trees?"

"But you can't possibly see through our hypocrisy when you're five years old!"
You've got to be at least twelve for that."

Eric Burgin

"Personally I can't wait to see what sort of mess
your generation makes of it!"

"When we say 'parents invited' we usually mean
sit and watch."

"I know it's expensive to bring up a kid.
Why come to me with your problems?"

"Next!"

"Do you have a set that doesn't make rude words?"

"What did you spoil his tiger trap for...?"

"I gotta write a poem about Dad. What rhymes with 'el dummo'?"

"I don't know where you learnt the patience to deal with kids, dear."

*"I don't really want to sneak on Benjamin, Miss Williams,
but really it was me who got that 9/10 Well Done."*

"Charlie Jackson's daughter only charges half that an hour for tuition."

"Bad news, Daddy — Mom's crushed by the suburban syndrome, you're taxed out of existence and I can't read."

"I don't think it's to do with your begetting an infant prodigy, Dad, so much as it's to do with you being stupid."

"Come in and get your tea quickly — Dad wants help with his homework."

"These are last year's reports."

"I've got my school report Dad — you didn't do very well."

"You can do your own homework next time!"

"Teacher says if I don't do well at school,
I'll end up like you."

"How come I never hear you say 'please' and 'thank-you'?"

"Off to join a commune for the middle-aged petit-bourgeoisie, that's where!"

"It's always the same — every time I tell him to shut up and listen to my advice based on a lifetime's experiences, I realise I haven't had any."

*"Can you imagine what it will be like in a few years' time —
I'll be slopping around the house full of pills, and you'll be wondering
where you went wrong, plus the fact that we won't be able to communicate..."*

"He won't be long Mom — he's just having a smoke behind the garage."

"Now, this is what I want next Christmas."

"I put that fish you brought home, Dad, in the fishbowl
and they swallowed it whole."

"These mock exam results are awful.
Heaven knows what your father is going to pretend to do to you!"

TONI GOFFE

"Can you afford to keep my daughter in the
drug habit she's accustomed to?"

"*Saying the bogeyman will get him doesn't seem to have too much effect these days.*"

"You learn that in a family-run business some procedures are handled differently."

"....with yellowy tufts and in front of them three more browny tufts, a twig and four silvery blue pebbles... To the right I remember there were two thistles and some long grass next to a rotting branch with fungus on it, which of course was in front of the chickweed with the unusual fronds on it... Aye, Son. It's all changed around here since I were a lad... Even that patch of bog moss or was it swamp leaf under the skutch gra..."

Books in "The World's Greatest" series
($4.99 £2.99 paperback)

The World's Greatest Cat Cartoons
The World's Greatest Computer Cartoons
The World's Greatest Dad Cartoons
The World's Greatest Golf Cartoons

Books in the "Victim's Guide" series
($4.99 £2.99 paperback)

Award winning cartoonist Roland Fiddy sees the funny side to life's phobias, nightmares and catastrophes.

The Victim's Guide to the Dentist
The Victim's Guide to the Doctor
The Victim's Guide to Middle Age

Books in the "Crazy World" series
($4.99 £2.99 paperback)

The Crazy World of Aerobics (Bill Stott)
The Crazy World of Cats (Bill Stott)
The Crazy World of Cricket (Bill Stott)
The Crazy World of Gardening (Bill Stott)
The Crazy World of Golf (Mike Scott)
The Crazy World of the Greens (Barry Knowles)
The Crazy World of The Handyman (Roland Fiddy)
The Crazy World of Hospitals (Bill Stott)
The Crazy World of Housework (Bill Stott)
The Crazy World of the Leaner Driver (Bill Stott)
The Crazy World of Love (Roland Fiddy)

The Crazy World of Marriage (Bill Stott)
The Crazy World of Rugby (Bill Stott)
The Crazy World of Sailing (Peter Rigby)
The Crazy World of Sex (David Pye)

Books in the "Fanatics" series
($4.99 £2.99 paperback)

The **Fanatic's Guides** are perfect presents for everyone with a hobby that has got out of hand. Eighty pages of hilarious black and white cartoons by Roland Fiddy

The Fanatic's Guide to the Bed
The Fanatic's Guide to Cats
The Fanatic's Guide to Computers
The Fanatic's Guide to Dads
The Fanatic's Guide to Diets
The Fanatic's Guide to Dogs
The Fanatic's Guide to Husbands
The Fanatic's Guide to Money
The Fanatic's Guide to Sex
The Fanatic's Guide to Skiing

Great Britain: Order these super books from your local bookseller or from Exley Publications Ltd, 16 Chalk Hill, Watford, Herts WD1 4BN. (Please send £1.30 to cover post and packaging on 1 book, £2.60 on 2 or more books.)